RHYME

&

REASON:

Facets

of a

Life

by

Claire Fluff Llewellyn

Copyright © 2020 Claire Fluff Llewellyn

ALL RIGHTS RESERVED.

No part of this publication may be reproduced, distributed, or transmitted in any form or by any means, including photocopying, recording, or other electronic or mechanical methods, without the prior written permission of the publisher, except in the case of brief quotations embodied in critical reviews and certain other non commercial uses permitted by copyright law. For permission requests and all other inquiries write to the publisher below.

Published by: Bloody Brit Press

bloodybritproductions@gmail.com

ISBN: 978-0-578-70603-0

https://www.facebook.com/britpoet

www.facebook.com/BloodyBritProductions

*Cover art by Claire Fluff Llewellyn. All images used are public domain, excluding the photographic image of, & taken by, Claire Fluff Llewellyn.

~ Dedication ~

For my grandparents Daisy and Howard Llewellyn, Nellie and Darcy Denyer. They taught me a lot about Life, Love, and Laughter. I miss them dearly. XXXX

Table of Contents

Introduction 6

LIFE! 9
- * Nostalgia 10
- * Poet For Sale 11
- * Clutching at Clouds 14
- * Extra Special 15
- * Extravertly Introvert 16
- * Liquor Slinger 18
- * Insomnia's Insanity 19
- * Sleep, Precious Sleep 20
- * I Am Cat, Hear Me Meow! 22
- * Disillusioned 23
- * Suffer in Silence 24
- * Out of the Darkness 26
- * Lessons 28
- * Rushing to Fail 30
- * The Forgotten 32
- * Trooping Through 33
- * Big Boss Man 34
- * Defiance 36
- * Isolation 37
- * Shopping, Corona Style 38

LOVE! 41
- * A Good Place to Start 42
- * Treasure 44
- * Grief Transcends 46
- * Where is Home 47
- * Perfect Daughter 48
- * Quicksand 50
- * Lift Me Up 51
- * White Picket Fence 52
- * Love Stinks 54
- * The Many Faces of Love 55

* Puppy Dog Eyes 56
* The Purest Form 57
* Friends 58
* Mother Earth 59

LAUGHTER! 61
   * Doctor Laughter 62
   * Going to Comic Con 63
   * The Ageing Curse 64
   * Simple Sally 68
   * Sheep Shagger aka Flossy's Revenge 72
   * Just Like the Movies! 76
    {The Twisted Tale of a Hollywood Hooker}
   * Santa Baby! 87

Acknowledgements 97

Also by Claire Fluff Llewellyn 98

About the Author 99

Introduction

Welcome to my world, won't you come on in!

You are about to embark on a journey into my mind, a scary place to be sure! But what is life, if not a little scary at times.

This collection of poetry is an 'everything and the kitchen sink' look at the many facets of life and the various emotions that bombard us throughout. At first glance it may appear a trifle depressing! As one of life's strugglers, I find writing as a creative release to be a very effective, and cheap, form of therapy. I was reluctant to publish some of these pieces, but the positive feedback I received on the more personal segment of my first book, 'LOVE is a KILLER', made me realise that there are people out there who can relate to my words and find comfort in the knowledge that they are not alone. So don't view those poems as purely negative! They are an outpouring of painful emotions reaching out to the like-minded with a virtual hug. I even offer some positive reinforcements!

That being said, if you're still with me, the overall theme of this book is the exploration of the many diverse factors that make up our lives: jobs, hobbies, relationships, family, friends, pets, mind chatter and the human condition. Not to mention a full spectrum of emotions to boot! These are divided into three sections: LIFE, LOVE, LAUGHTER. [Although some poems could fall under more than one category.]

I have no doubt that the 'LAUGHTER' portion of the book will be many people's favourite. You have to have a healthy balance to stay sane and a sense of humour is vital to our mental well being. I have to warn you though...my humour errs on the twisted side and can get a tad dark in places! I love to tell stories so some of these poems get quite lengthy and are mostly fictional, [and my penchant for horror is obvious].

So get ready for a roller-coaster of ups and downs, laughs and frowns. A cacophony of rhymes for these troubling times. I'll start you with a smile, limerick style!...

There once was a poet called Claire

Who liked to rhyme as a dare

But when challenged with *'orange'*

Her mind imploded

Now she sees that damn fruit everywhere!

Claire Fluff Llewellyn

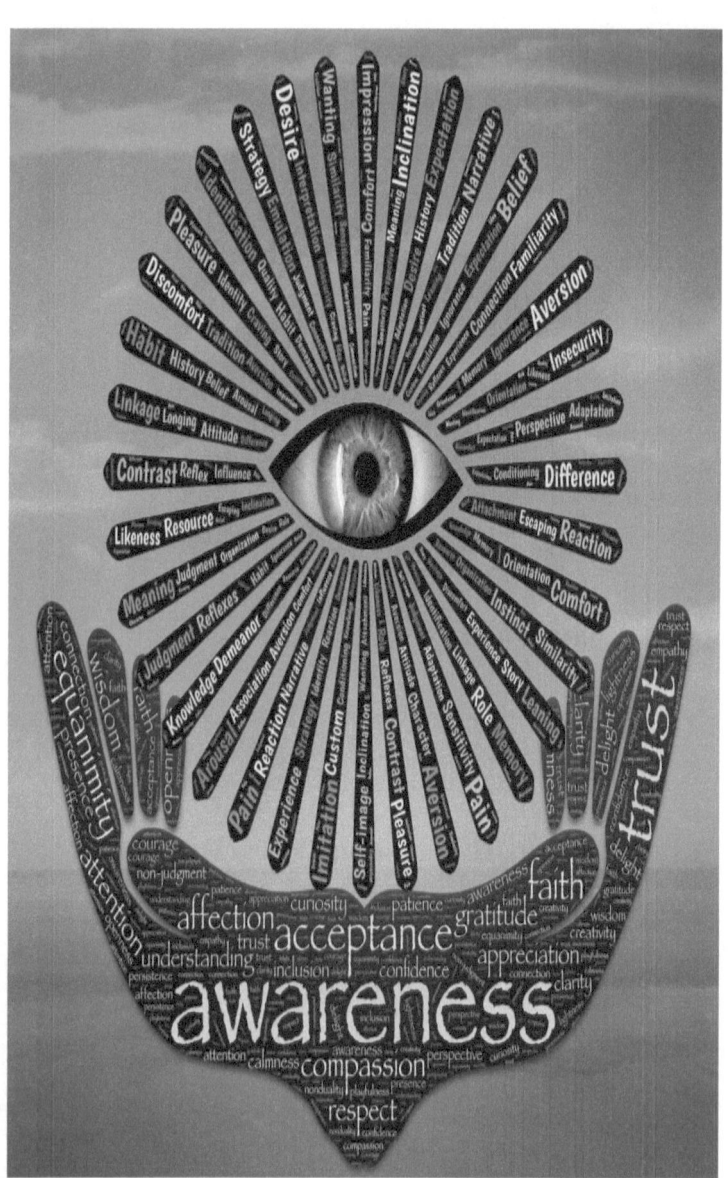

LIFE!

"Life can only be understood backwards; but it must be lived forwards." ~ Soren Kierkegaard

NOSTALGIA

Feeling nostalgic
Yearning for the past
How I wish I could turn back time

Mistakes I'd erase
I'm wiser these days
Never to repeat the crime

Live for today
Enjoy what you have
I think I've forgotten how!

Was the past all that?
Or do I just feel trapped?
Disappointed by the now

No going back
Only moving on
Forward to reinvention

Past is past!
Present can change
Future's ready for invention

POET FOR SALE

Can I sell you a rhyme, Sir?
One a penny, five a dime, Sir?
Or maybe three a nickel?
I'm really in a pickle!

Though creepy old guys
and sympathy buys
hurt my ego plenty.
I guess I should be flattered
as I'm worn and battered
and many years past twenty!

I hawk my words
to the literary herds
and seek their vain approval.
Hoping they will buy,
not pass on by
or entreat my prompt removal!

It's a hard knock life,
full of trouble and strife,
being a poem pushing pedlar.
But I'm an honest bird,
as good as my word,
not some conniving, low-life meddler.

If you buy from me
I can guarantee,
I'll put a smile on your face.
I'll write you a verse
if you open your purse
or wallet, whichever's the case.

I won't steer you wrong,
my words are like songs
filled with pain and passion!
And humour too,
for when you're blue!
They'll grow on you after a fashion.

I could sell you a sonnet
that'll lift anyone's bonnet,
if your purpose is to woo.
There's nothing to lose
and a bounty to choose,
just pick what best suits you.

So what do you say, Sir?
Don't walk away, Sir!
A gal can't live on fresh air!
What about you, Miss?
Don't walk away too, Miss!
Surely you've a penny to spare?

Who will buy a rhyme?
One a penny, five a dime!

*Video performance can be viewed here:
https://youtu.be/xJzUvurDqIM

CLUTCHING AT CLOUDS

Clutching at clouds
Empty promises
Heartbeats in shallow words

Read aloud
Sacred prophecies
Spoken, never heard

Dream a dream
Live a fantasy
Never treading solid ground

Life it seems
Harsh reality
Pot of gold, not found

EXTRA SPECIAL

The life of an extra is wait, wait, wait
But there's no better way to make dough
Sit down, stand up, stand tall, stand straight
Rolling, background go

You may see big names
But if you think you'll be one, stop!
This won't bring you fame
You're just a walking prop

But being on the set
Is a thrill, it must be said
It's easy money yet
You even get well fed!

So I'll wait for my cue
To walk onto the scene
Do what I'm told to do
And maybe I'll be seen . . .

On the TV or big screen
So I can stand up and yell
"That's ME, see me lean?"
'Cause I'm an '*Extra*' special gal!

EXTRAVERTLY INTROVERT

I may seem gregarious
on the surface,
that's just my performer's mask.
I can natter all day,
I got plenty to say!
But being sociable's a draining task.

I can stand on the stage,
address a large crowd,
even sing with a Rock n' Roll band!
I'll hide my anxiety
when out in society,
I'll do what my ego demands.

But I'd much rather hide
away from the cliques
and their ever judgmental eyes.
And I don't need peeps
who give me the creeps
with their sycophantic lies!

Don't get me wrong
or think me standoffish
if I sometimes appear withdrawn.
Just need a moment to breathe,
when trepidation's relieved,
I'll be back on form.

I'm naturally shy,
though I've dressed otherwise,
and it's so easy to revert.
To validate my enigma
and be introspective without stigma . . .

        I'm EXTRAVERTLY *introvert!*

LIQUOR SLINGER

Liquor slinger
Booze jockey
Spirit pusher
Shot tottie

At weekends you will find me
at your local grocery store,
serving up free samples.
So stop by for a pour.

Wine, beer, spirits;
all for you to try!
I'll even educate you;
you don't *have* to buy!

Some pleasant conversation;
my accent breaks the ice.
A little stiff libation
makes shopping twice as nice!

Whiskey pimpin'
Tipple tipper
Cocktail dolly
Slinging liquor

INSOMNIA'S INSANITY

So I get to thinking,
it's night and I'm drinking
coffee when I should be sleeping
but my mind is keeping
me awake....
How many licks *does* it take
to get to the centre of a Tootsie Pop?
Now my brain just won't stop!
Why is the meaning of life 42?
I wish I knew!
But if I count 42 sheep,
will *that* help me sleep?
Well, I guess not
as I stare at the clock,
just lying in bed
then into my head
pops a familiar song
and I sing along
the few words that I know
and off I go
repeating again and again....
I'm going insane!!
Tossing and turning,
the words keep returning!
And suddenly without warning...
It's morning!

SLEEP, PRECIOUS SLEEP

Need sleep, precious sleep
The drain, the *drain!*
Without it, I weep
The pain, the *pain!*

You kept me awake
For shame, for *shame!*
The bed, you did shake
Refrain, *refrain!*

Now I must rise
No time, no *time!*
Light hurts my eyes
The crime, the *crime!*

Head hurts me so
So bad, so *bad!*
But I must go
I'm mad, I'm *mad!*

Mood very black
Fatigue, *fatigue!*
I want my bed back
I need, I *need!*

Coffee all day
Caffeine, *caffeine!*
Awake I must stay
So mean, so *mean!*

Home I arrive
So tired, so *tired!*
On my bed I dive
I'm wired, I'm *WIRED!!*

I AM CAT, HEAR ME MEOW

Meow, I need food
Meow, I need fuss
MEOW, *still no food!*
This *meow* is a cuss

I see you sleeping, human!
But I am wide awake
If you ignore me, human!
The more noise I will make

Can't you feel me walking over you?
As you lie in your bed
For your attention I'm overdue
So I'll paw at your head

Your ancient peoples worshipped me
They knew how to treat me right
For I'm a God and you must serve me
Or you'll not sleep tonight!

Listen to me, human!
M*eow, meow, MEOW!*
You're *my* slave, human!
How'd you like me now?

DISILLUSIONED

Who am I?
What have I become?
How did I get here?
What have I done?

A middle-aged nobody
Wanted to be somebody
Body gone to pot
Did I miss my last shot?

Wasted time
Wasted youth
Wasted life!

Lost motivation
Lost hope
Lost cause!

Accomplishments zero
Disillusionment maxed!
Apathy, the hero
When dreams are axed

SUFFER IN SILENCE

Darkness swirling, enveloping your mind
Light and joy your eyes can't find
Heart so heavy, sinking down
Lips upended, brow in frown

Raw emotion that people fear
Passion and pain no one will hear
Suffer in silence
'Cause no-one wants to hear it
Suffer in silence
'Cause people fear it

Put on a front
It's what they want
Wear a 'happy' mask
So they won't ask

Suffer in silence
Hide feelings away
Suffer in silence
Don't display
Raw emotion that people fear
Anguish that they won't hear

Silence is your only friend
It's all silence in the end!...

But at the end of the tunnel there *is* light
And within you is the strength to fight
Don't suffer in silence
Don't hide that sad face
Don't suffer in silence
You can't be replaced!

OUT OF THE DARKNESS

Into the darkness
There is no light
The end of the tunnel is black

It swallows me whole
No strength to fight
Limbs like lead hold me back

I feel no release
The grip holds me tight
My heart under constant attack

Compassion come find me!
A warm smile in my sight
A shoulder to burden the slack

A hand, an ear
Understanding my plight
Kindness this coffin crack

Empathy, my saviour!
Your support give me flight
Released and never look back

Out of the darkness . . .
>*Into the light*

Out of the darkness . . .
>*Into the light*

LESSONS

Teach me how to live
Teach me how to fly
Teach me to forgive
Teach me not to cry

Teach me not to hate
Teach me to be strong
Teach me how to wait
Teach me right from wrong

Teach me not to judge
Teach me to be fair
Teach me not to hold a grudge
Teach me how to care

Teach me how to love
Teach me to be true
Teach me how to rise above
Teach me that each day is new

Teach me to be humble
Teach me to be meek
Teach me not to grumble
Teach me to turn the other cheek

Teach me that I am loved
Teach me to see the good
Teach me dignity, when I am shoved
Teach me how to be understood

These are lessons we must learn,
to help us through the pain.
To help us heal the burn,
when life brings fire or rain.

Learn that we all have needs
Learn that we all have flaws
Learn compassion over greed
Learn that kindness opens doors

RUSHING TO FAIL

Always in a rush
'Cause I'm always late
Procrastination
Tempting fate
Afraid to fail
Failing to win
Successful betrayal
A losers grin

Wasting time
No time to waste
Sedentary
Fast-paced
Yo-yo brain
Bi-polar spin
Up but down
Internal din

Placing blame
"Can't be my fault!"
Stagnation
End result
"Motivation,
Where art thou?"
Justification
Need it now

Saboteur
My own, am I
Over-thinking
Life speeds by
Desperation
Epic derail
In my own way . . .

        Rushing to fail!

THE FORGOTTEN

Will I leave my mark upon this earth?
When I am gone, will my life have been worth
anything? . . .

                                              to anyone?

Or just another corpse to move along!
Your day is done; you've sang your song
to everyone . . .

                                              and no one!

No lasting trace; no works of art.
No resting place within the hearts
of anyone . . .

                                              not a one!

I am the hidden in plain view.
I am the many and the few.
I am everyone . . .

                                              and no one!

TROOPING THROUGH

Through rejection
I plough through
A trooper till the end!

Though wounded deep
My heart stays true
Strengthened by a friend

BIG BOSS MAN

Clueless, immature, maniacal man in charge
Arrogant, ignorant little man
Know it all, know nothing
Fascist dictator, woman hater
Big bottom line
I draw the line
At your subversive methods

Your way or the highway!
A road I don't want to travel
I'd rather pound gravel
Than bow to your commands
And ridiculous demands
That barely seem legit
But you just won't quit!

Blue collar, white collar
It's all about the dollar
That goes into *your* pocket
From the sweat of the working class
Who fight day to day
To get by on their pay
While you just sit on your ass!

The worst, you hire
The best, you fire
Your will is LAW
With an *"untouchable"* air
You rule without care
So help those who dare
Criticise a flaw

Surviving your reign is the toughest test
Of anyone's metal
While the powerless settle
Afraid to speak their truth
For fear of losing their roof
The rebels grow wise
Plotting your demise

Thoughts of revolution
Could be a solution
For the 99%'s woe
Make you eat crow
Now that would be a show
I would very much like to see
Save a front row seat for me!

DEFIANCE

I *won't* be told
that I'm too old,
or I'm NOT this or that!
And I *won't* be shamed
for the pounds I've gained,
if society deems me fat!

Your expectations
are exaggerations
of unrealistic goals!
Fallacy
breeds fantasy,
and a plot line full of holes!

The toughest critic
of myself is ME,
so pleasing YOU ain't squat!
If I pass MY test,
you've got the best;
trust me, that's a lot!

Still unconvinced?
Not surprising, since
I don't fit in with your plan!
But I'll stay strong;
sing my own song,
for *defiant*, I am!

ISOLATION

The sun is shining,
but I'm feeling blue.
Let down by people
who can't be true.
Self absorption's
a modern plague.
We're all infected
in different ways.

Sun's still shining;
I'm still blue!
Missing people
I never knew.
Isolation's
a state of mind.
A desert island
left behind.

SHOPPING, CORONA STYLE

In the supermarket, I frown
So many shelves empty and bare
The World has become a ghost town
And no loo roll anywhere!

No zombie hoards, just hoarders
Who already cleaned out the store
Like a pack a savage marauders
What do they need all that toilet paper for?

With a scarf around my face like a bandit
Intent on scoring my precious supplies
Face starts to itch, I can't stand it!
Damn my unprotected, allergy eyes

A recorded voice over the tannoy
Repeats "For your safety keep six feet apart!"
As I rush for the last pack of Chips-Ahoy
And triumphantly lob it in my cart

A few cans of vegetables later
I look at my pathetic collection
Luckily it's only me I have to cater
For, with this apocalyptic menu selection

Maybe I could use some liquor
To help me get through this ordeal
If I'm drunk will it end any quicker?
The whole thing's just so surreal

I must not forget the pet food
I hope that they haven't sold out
Furry friends really do lighten your mood
They're my saving grace no doubt

On to the cleaning goods section
Wiped clean of all sanitizer
But I still have my soap-on-a-rope for protection
I think the virus will be none the wiser

Lastly to the produce aisle
Oh and tea, lest I forget
I like a banana once in a while
And now I think I'm all set

'**X**' marks the spot at the checkout
A reminder to keep your distance
Grab your groceries and get out
But just stay home if you have low resistance

LOVE!

"Where there is love there is life." ~
Mahatma Gandhi

A GOOD PLACE TO START

Wear compassion
like it's fashion.
Be proud to show it!
Let other's know it
doesn't cost a dime
to spend time
spreading love not hate!
It's not too late
to heal each other,
we're all sisters/brothers
of the same Mother Earth.
Aren't we ALL worth
equal affection
and positive direction?

Time to unite
and win the fight
against those that divide us
and deride us.
In fear they invest
and those who ingest
buy into the delusion
fooled by an illusion
of impending doom
from a foreign womb.
We must resist
and not enlist
in some dictator's entourage
causing humanity's sabotage!

Can love conquer all?
Is the gesture too small?
It's asking a lot
and a cure it is not
but if we open our hearts
it's a good place to start.

TREASURE

Treasure
What gives you pleasure
Simple things we take for granted
Ignorant dreams of bliss, implanted

Nurture
What can hurt you
They suffer now from your neglect
You suffer later from their disrespect

Through pain, you'll learn
Feel shame, the burn
It's a bitter pill that's hard to swallow
Act today, don't repent tomorrow

Careful when you take advice
Be sure your source, think twice
One wrong move could cost you dear
Good intentions won't see you clear

Sadness
Replaces gladness
The joy you shared has come to a stop
Too late now to turn back the clock

Regretting
Never forgetting
Realization of mistakes you've made
No erasing the price they paid

Sorrow
Becomes tomorrow
Empty feeling inside you growing
Tell yourself there was no way of knowing

Through pain, you'll learn
Feel shame, the burn
It's a bitter pill that's hard to swallow
Act *today*, don't repent tomorrow!

GRIEF TRANSCENDS

As you grieve
You must believe
That there's a better place

Love never ends
It just transcends
Through time and space

Celebrate the life of the one you loved
As you heal
You will feel
Their warmth from above

Know in your heart
They'll always be a part
Of you forever
Treasure the memories you shared together

LOVE
                       NEVER
                                        ENDS

It just ...

                       TRANSCENDS!

WHERE IS HOME

Home is a feeling,
more than a place.
You can feel *'at home'* with a person
or in a place that's not where you live!
It's the feeling
of comfort, safety, nurturing.

No matter where you roam,
within your heart is home.

PERFECT DAUGHTER

Am I now
Or have I ever been
The perfect daughter?
Do I do
Or have I ever done
What my parents said I oughta?

NO

Do I make
Or have I ever made
The best decisions?
Do I meet
Or have I ever met
My parents' visions?

NO

Do I show
Have I always shown
Appreciation for what they do?
Do I say
Have I always said
The words, *'I Love You'*?

NO

Do I know
Have I always known
That they do their best for me?
Do I think
Have I always thought
That they're the best parents they can be?

YES

                      I LOVE YOU

QUICKSAND

Depression like quicksand, dragging me down
Weight of the world helping me drown
Is your love strong enough to set me free
Or will you walk away and bury me?

LIFT ME UP

Lift me up from the mire
Send your love down the wire
Don't treat me like a pariah
I'm human!
          … just like you!

All it takes is understanding
When life gets rough and too demanding
Stop judgemental social branding
Be human!
          … kind and true

WHITE PICKET FENCE

I do not suffer fools gladly
If you want me to love you truly, madly
Then just be you, no need for pretence
I'm not looking for a white picket fence
It's really not hard to gain my favour
I'm not looking for a Saviour
Don't be a dick, don't cheat or lie
Don't be the one who makes me cry
Treat me like I'm worth your time
Loving me ain't no crime

Don't want a villain in disguise
No Prince Charming full of lies
Not looking for the Holy Grail
But I ain't no cheap piece of tail
Respect me and earn my trust
That's just a basic must
If you're just looking for a toy
Then move on down the road, boy!
I'm too damn tired to play that game
Need someone who feels the same

But I must be honest with myself
And not afraid to sit on that shelf
For time spent alone is not time wasted
Stronger for the poison fruit not tasted
Enjoying your own company
Is a very healing place to be
For learning to love oneself
Is essential for emotional health
So I'll be patient, come what may
And wait 'till the right one happens my way

LOVE STINKS

Love sucks, love stinks,
pushes you to the brink
of intellectual extinction
when there's no clear distinction
between love and lust!

Adrenalized hormones
reacting to pheromones
fuels carnal desire,
sets hearts a-fire
and scrambles the brain!

Then comes the pain …
when the flame is extinguished
and the feelings distinguished:
It was lust all along!
Time to move along.

THE MANY FACES OF LOVE

Cupid may wear many disguises
Love comes in many guises
You love your life partner
But not the same as your mom!
At least, that is, not where I'm from

I love chocolate, but it doesn't love me!
That's not the same, you see
You can't *truly* love an inanimate object!
It's the love for another sentient being
When reciprocated, is spiritually freeing

I love my friends like I love my brother
But that's not the same as I love my lover!
I'm not 'in love' with my friends and family
That's the feeling you get looking into the eyes
Of that 'special one' who give you butterflies

I love most creatures, great and small
Especially the cutest and fluffiest of all
But I'll not bed or wed my pet dog, Snuffles!
That's totally not my meaning, Jack
When I say I love an animal in the sack!

So give love, but in appropriate ways!
And love will brighten your darkest days

PUPPY DOG EYES

Nothing melts the heart faster than
> *puppy dog eyes*

Nor drains the wallet faster than
> *puppy dog eyes*

If you fall for the master of those
> *puppy dog eyes*

Your heart and wallet will be broke!

THE PUREST FORM

When you see a baby, puppy or kitten
Are you instantly smitten?
Do you smile and feel all aglow?
If *"Yes"*, then you know
Pure love, it's unconditional
Not transactional
No strings, rope or chord
It is its own reward

Helping those who cannot ...
Your action means a lot
And their appreciation
Gives you a warm, fuzzy sensation
That lifts your spirit and mind
It costs nothing to be kind
So let kindness be the norm
And love in its purest form

FRIENDS

New friends, old friends
Silver and gold friends
Feathered friends, furry friends
Friends near and far

Cherish them, protect them
Nurture and respect them
Support them, enjoy them
Wherever they are

MOTHER EARTH

Our Great Green Earth
That once was
The Mother
To us all
Lies dying
At our feet
Choked
By our hands
Matricide
By pesticide
Chemical soup
Plastic pollution . . .

But there's a solution!
Not too late
To recycle
Reconnect
Harmonize
Empathize
Clean up our act,
our oceans,
our planet!
Healthy Mother
Healthy child
We *all* win!

LAUGHTER!

"Always laugh when you can. It is cheap medicine." ~ Lord Byron

DOCTOR LAUGHTER

Try a shot of laughter!
You'll feel better thereafter
No needle to cause you pain
You'll be happy once again!
You don't even need insurance!
I give you my assurance
That this will make you smile
If only for a while
If something makes you miserable
Just think of something risible
Like grandpas in pink tutus
Wearing giant clown shoes!
It won't cost you any money
To think of something funny
This is my medical advice
And cheap at half the price!

GOING TO COMIC CON

Going to Comic Con
Sure to be lots of fun

There'll be grown men with their underwear
Outside their trousers
Women with costumes barely there
Geek snake arousers

Cosplay, Anime, even Furries
Are all welcome here
Nerds, Geeks, Costumed Freaks
Mingle with no fear

Come on out to Comic Con
You're sure to have lots of fun

Meet celebs of books and screen
Get autographs and photo-ops
Comics galore, a nerd's wet dream
Imagination never stops

See you there at Comic Con
We're going have lots of fun!

THE AGEING CURSE

Hair today, gone tomorrow
Widow's peak, spinster's sorrow
Crows feet and hammer toes
Droopy jowls and hairy nose

Sounds like a witch's spell
Growing old can be hell
No amount of fancy lotion
Can reverse this bitch's potion

Memory getting worse
Such is this ageing curse
Bloated belly and failing eyes
I do believe the camera lies

Mirror, mirror on the wall
Who the **** you gonna call?
When some old crone stares back at you!
This reflection can't be true

Another birthday rolls around
Another year, another pound
Or two, or three, or several more
I can't even touch the floor!

Bending might throw out my back
Too much stress means heart attack
They say, "Exercise is the cure!"
Getting out of bed, makes me sore!

Gone are my clubbing days
When I was in my 'Rock Chick' phase
Now it's for comfort that I settle
A fashion choice that's so un-metal!

Can't handle more than two drinks
This getting old shit really stinks
Interrupted by my weak bladder
A night of fun just makes me sadder

And triple my recovery time
It'll be three days before I'm fine
The stamina I had in my youth
Is shot to hell, ain't that the truth!

My age clubs called 'Grab a Granny'
Not a place to grab a fanny!
[For those who live in the land of Trump,
I ain't talking about one's rump!]

The 'meat market', I do not miss
The mating dances, the charmers hiss
'Cause experience makes you wise
That part of ageing I don't despise

Now I'd rather curl up with a juicy book
A dog, and maybe someone who can cook
My patience becoming as thin as my hair
Don't fancy me? I really don't care

My libido has gone to pot
Sales on Crocs, get me hot!
No longer lust for frequent sex
Such is this evil hex

Hot flashes and sagging tits
Ageing really is the pits
Spider and varicose veins
Increasing daily aches and pains

Though thankful for no more bleeding
'Cause I really don't feel like breeding
My mood flips from tears to rage
Bloody hormones, a curse at any age!

No magic wand can turn back time
So I'll convince myself this is my prime
I guess life could dish out far worse
Than the inevitable ageing curse

I'll just sit on my porch, stifling a yawn
Yelling at the kids to "Get off my lawn!"
These young 'uns just don't have a clue
That the ageing curse will get them too!

SIMPLE SALLY

All Simple Sally simply wanted
Was a plain and simple life
Free from heartache, free from pain
Free from trouble and strife

Really didn't seem a lot
Not much for a girl to ask
But breaking free, seemed to be
A tremendously difficult task

She quit her job at the factory
Sold all her stuff online
To her landlord, gave her notice
Told her boyfriend she needed some time

She found a house on Ebay
It really was a steal!
She bought it, not hesitating
The listing sounded ideal:

'Two bedroom seaside cottage
Cozy, charming and quaint
Move right in, no taxes or liens
Just needs some TLC and paint'

Simple Sally was excited
A place to call her own
Free from hustle, free from bustle
The seeds of her dreams were sown

She packed her simple belongings
A few necessities she didn't sell
To her landlord, gave the finger
Told her neighbours to go to hell

After two days of endless driving
She finally arrived at her place
Picture in hand, didn't quite match
Excitement drained from her face

A note on the door said: *"Welcome,
Under the mat is the key"*
She entered her home, most anxious
Afraid of what she would see

It really was a shambles
In desperate need of repair
A lick of paint, what bollocks
She fought back tears of despair

Sparse furnishings were scattered
And a futon and cleaning supplies
Feeling deflated, exhaustion took over
She lay down and closed her eyes

Next day she awoke with gusto
Determined to fix up her home
To the stores she went, defiant
Returned with a garden gnome!

She sat and stared in frustration
She had to get out of her funk
To the rescue, music from Mötorhead
To the beat she cleared out the junk

End of the day she was knackered
But her optimism did increase
Rubbish all gone, scrubbed up quite well
With some serious elbow grease

With YouTube as her teacher
She patched up here and there
She worked hard, harder than ever
But finished with money to spare!

It really wasn't as simple
As Simple Sally dreamed it would be
Poured blood and sweat, many tears too
But perseverance was the key

Now Sally's quite contented
Proud of herself and her home
Simple's not simple, hard work rewards
Now she's chillin' with her garden gnome
[who she named Lemmy]

SHEEP SHAGGER aka Flossy's Revenge!

There wanders restless a little sheep
Whose virgin wool she prays to keep
But lo there sneaks a horny Celt
With Velcro gloves and utility belt

As the degenerate oaf climbs over the stile
He steps into a stinking fresh pile
Of 'gardener's gold', rich sheep manure
The smell of the country was never so pure!

He curses as he shakes the shit off his welly
He's never encountered droppings so smelly!
What on earth has this sheep consumed?
Undeterred, his stalking resumes

With a Muttley grin and eyes that are glossy
He stealthily approaches the lone sheep, Flossy
Then he notices the grass beneath her is red
And she is grazing on a *human* head!

The head belongs to a bloke called Dave
Who he met last week at a Young Farmer's rave
But where the hell is the rest him?
Sheep don't tear people limb from limb!

Quite disturbed by this gruesome sight
He contemplates on poor Dave's plight
Though his bestial urges know no bounds
Until over the hill came some frightful sounds

An army of sheep, out for blood
Lead by a ram who's pounding the mud
He has jet black fleece and glowing red eyes
His commanding bleats like savage war cries

Little Flossy, unstirred, continues to munch
Whilst the petrified pervert looses his lunch
The ram lowers his head, charges down the hill
Spurred on by bleating chants of "KILL"

Unable to run and nowhere to hide
The ram connects with the Celt's backside
And the tosser is tossed into a hedge of thorns
Thanks to the power of those mighty black horns

He struggles to free himself of the brambles
That rip his clothing and start to strangle
But better off scratched than ending up dead
With a sheep chowing down on your severed head

He hears the murderous flock approaching
Bent on revenge for his encroaching
Onto their turf with intentions so vile
Looking for a lonely young sheep to defile

With skin tearing force he sees himself clear
Of his thorny captor, but his eyes fill with fear
As impaled on a tree is his best mate, Owen
Stomach ripped open, intestines flowing

In a panic he slips in something wet and slick
Landing on the remains of a prick named Mick
Though his mangled face is missing a nose
He's recognisable from his chavish clothes

Struck with sudden, violent regurgitation
Nauseated by such sick mutilation
The deplorable droog fails to see
Little Flossy approaching, nonchalantly

She slipped through a small hole in the hedge
Just big enough through which she could wedge
Cheered on by a chorus of bloodthirsty sheep
Eager to end this cretinous creep

Flossy bleats out a greeting, sweet as you please
Then sinks her teeth into one of his knees
He howls in pain and abject horror
Realising he won't see tomorrah!

He thought his shenanigans would be a riot
Not knowing the sheep had changed their diet
To include the flesh of scum such as he
Now he'll reap the bloody revenge of Flossy!

JUST LIKE THE MOVIES:
{THE TWISTED TALE OF A HOLLYWOOD HOOKER}

Lusty Lisa was a Hollywood hooker
Once a good looker
But fell on hard times

She could've been a contender
But the ultimate bender
Led her to a life of crime

"I'm really not bad, just drawn that way!"
Is what she'd say
When busted by the law

But stupid really is as stupid does
'Cause no-one really loves
A coked out, ageing whore!

So she worked the street
Trying to compete
With others in her trade

"Can't you see I'm walking here!"
She made it clear
That she would not be played!

A John said, "Hi!"
From a car close by
She descended, "Are you talkin' to me?"

John: "You can call me Mister Tibbs!
And I'm claiming dibs
on your rentable pussey!"

"Well, you got me at 'hello'.
Now where shall we go?"
He replied, "Ain't no place like my home!

Fasten your seatbelt, it'll be a bumpy night!"
And he buckled her tight
She responded with a lustful moan

To the ocean they did drive
And when they did arrive
He escorted her to a small pontoon

"I think you need a bigger boat!"
It was a tiny house afloat
Waiting there under the moon

He cried, "Oh Stella, *Stella!*"
She countered, "Listen here, fella!
You can call me whatever you will!

But Lisa's my name,
and I'll play your game
as long as you pay your bill!"

He pushed her aboard
Before losing his gourd
"That'll do, ho. That'll do."

It was roomy inside
With places to hide
Bathed in a garish hue

"Ignore that man behind the curtain!"
Then she knew for certain
That something wasn't right

"You gotta show me the money,
if you want a threesome, honey!
One. Million. Dollars. I'll even spend the night!"

"We gotta problem!", he said to the peeper
"She thinks I am a creeper!
Well, that Rosebud ain't heard nothin' yet!"

He threw her on the bed
She hit her vacant head
And darkness cast its eerie net

"She's *alive!* She's *alive!*"
He quipped as she revived
The peeper pointed a camera at her face

"Are you ready for your close-up?
Or do you want to coke-up?"
She wished she could reach her can of mace!

"I may be a ho!
I'm still a person though!"
She growled into the phallic lens

The men were unperplexed
She became more vexed
"And I have some burly biker friends!"

The peeper scoffed, "Frankly, my dear,
let me make this clear!
For threats I don't give a damn!

My primary goal
is to save your wretched soul.
For your Father, I am!

This is an intervention
for your spiritual re-invention!"
He continued his pious diatribe

"I shall purge your vile flaws
and baptise you in my cause!
My righteous love you will imbibe."

He handed the camera to her John
And prepared to *get it on'!*
Mr Tibbs set the camera to record

She quickly tried to think
On the bed she did shrink
Mustering what strength she could afford

"Get your paws off me, you damned dirty chimp!
You ain't my f'in pimp!"
Is all she could really think to say

This was just too damn bizarre
And pushing her too far
She'd never heard of this kink in role play!

"Lisa, you're tearing me apart!
Would you break your father's heart?
You must repent and not resist!

Let my seed cleanse you
and spiritually ascend you.
I'm afraid I really must insist!"

"I've never met my dad.
I heard he was a cad!"
She tried to subvert this sordid scene

"You don't care my mother died!
Or all the nights I cried!
Where the hell have you been?"

"My Precious, I'm here now!
And it is my solemn vow
to rid you of those demons of the flesh!

When I saw the light,
I swore to make it right.
To do that our bodies must mesh!

So say hello to my special friend!
And together we will mend
your broken morality.

Let your father in
to banish all your sin!
And fix your wanton personality."

With some aggressive cajoling
The camera still rolling
He mounted, and pinned her beneath

"Heeeere's *Daddy!*"
He thrust, but had he
Known her vagina had teeth!...

He would have thought twice
Before claiming *this* vice
He squealed like a pig

Coin in the slot
In for the money shot
Mr Tibbs didn't twig

That this writhing reaction
Was not satisfaction
And the peeper's pecker was gone!

As the camera zoomed in
Blood sprayed onto his chin
And he realised something's quite wrong!

He gasped, "*Inconceivable!*
It's quite unbelievable!"
Mr Tibbs was shaken, not stirred

"Beauty killed the beast!"
So he thought at least
Then the peeper's groaning was heard

"But I'm not dead!"
And he rolled off the bed
A bloody stump where his penis had been

"It's just a flesh wound!", she scoffed
As his blood sprayed aloft
"It's not the worst that I've seen.

Sometimes, dead is better!"
She started to get wetter
And gave Mr Tibbs the eye

Mr Tibbs freaked out
He had no doubt
That's not the way he wanted to die

"I have it under control,
I only chomp on assholes
who choose to disrespect me!

My life is tough
and when things get rough
it's the only thing that protects me!"

The peeper groaned once more
He was bleeding out on the floor
"How can you do this to your own dad?

My Lisa Marie
you complete me!
Can't you see my intentions weren't bad!"

"I'm Lisa Renata
of the Vagina Dentata!
And it seems you have me mistaken.

For that I'm glad
although I'm still mad,
I saved your real daughter being taken!

I'm no prude,
but you're one sick dude!
You got what you had coming!"

Mr Tibbs backed away
From this gruesome display
Turned and started running

The peeper struggled for breath
And was very close to death
When he offered her a financial reward

To save his sorry ass
She gave a hard pass
Dragged him out and slid him overboard

Before he sank out of sight
He put up a good fight
She encouraged him to "Just keep swimming!"

Then it was "Hasta la vista!
Not sorry, Mister!"
And she finally felt she was winning

Now Lisa owns her own home
And is free to roam
Wherever she may sail

But don't try to find her
Or she'll gladly remind ya
Of this not so *'Hollywood'* tale!

SANTA BABY!

Christmas; a time of stress for Jimmy's mother
So glad was she that there was no other
One brat like Jimmy was quite enough
Not to mention the financial strain was tough
For a single parent it's a trying season
Kids don't understand your reason

To the mall she took the boy
Every year for a cheap new toy
Given by some creepy impostor
Taken off the unemployment roster
Those red-suited fakes made her wince
And she's been stone cold sober since . . .

'Twas seven years past on a Christmas Eve
That little Jimmy was conceived
In the broom closet at the office party
She was drunk and he was hearty
All she really can remember
Is Santa came early that December

All were costumed for the occasion
She an angel with liquid persuasion
But no-one knew who was her mate
The red-suited sinner who sealed her fate
Was it some perverted game?
He left as quickly as he came

At first she thought it was her boss
A sleazy flirt who needed to floss
But he was macking on another
As she engaged this subversive lover
The quintessential *'Secret Santa'*
Leaves a gift, but no telling banter . . .

So she became a secret Santa hater
Still bitter these seven years later
Seven years of constant bad luck
Because of that sneaky closet ****
If only she could find a way
To track him down and make him pay

Why she'd give him all kinds of abuse
But her bitterness turned her into a recluse
Never tempting to find a more stable lover
Little Jimmy would be no-one's brother
So Jimmy remained a fatherless child
Which made him grow unruly and wild

Lost in her woes, she paid no attention
When little Jimmy's name was mentioned
It was his turn to sit on Santa's knee
He charged the scene and bounced with glee
On the fat, red man with the jolly veneer
Who looked at Jimmy with a menacing sneer

"Have you been naughty, or have you been nice?
Santa shouldn't have to ask twice!"
Little Jimmy thought he looked weird
Something evil beneath that foul beard
He tugged at the matted mess on his chin
It didn't budge. Santa started to grin

Jimmy leapt from his lap and ran to mom
"That can't be Santa! Where is *he* from?
Mommy, I think he's a baddy!"
"Hush now son, he could be your daddy!"
Santa and Jimmy stared in surprise
She hugged her boy with tears in her eyes

Santa, spooked by that very notion
Made for the door, causing a commotion
The kids waiting in line started to bawl
As Santa legged it out of the mall
He ducked in a bar to catch his breath
Being pinned with a kid would be his death

Jimmy joined the other kids in crying
Why oh why had his mother been lying
About Santa and his absent father?
Who he heard was Satan but is likely rather
Some bum who plays Santa once a year
And reeks of too much Christmas cheer!

The bartender welcomed the winded red man
"This one's on me. You see, I'm a fan!"
The place was decked out like Santa's Grotto
With several mall Santas already quite blotto
He started to relax and enjoy himself
As he eyed up a server dressed liked an elf

An elf gave Jimmy *two* gifts and a smile!
Hoping to shut him up for a while
His mother almost got into a fight
With a parent who thought it only right
That their child should get the same as her boy
As they were next in line for Santa's toy

Embarrassed that her momentary lapse
Caused the festive gathering to collapse
Into total and utter disarray
She ushered Jimmy quietly out of the fray
And hurried to the parking lot
Telling Jimmy to be thankful for what he got

As they headed for home, Jimmy still sobbing
Her mind was distracted and head throbbing
When suddenly staggering out of the bar
And into the path of her beat up old car
Came that same Santa who from them had fled
"Serves him right if he's lying there dead!"

She thought as she stopped and got out to look
But the drunken lout just seemed to be shook
As he wavered and groggily got up on his feet
A slew of soused Santas converged on the street
They stumbled to help their fallen brother
And mumbled abuse at Jimmy's Mother

She stood there aghast, growing ever more mad
The thought that any *one* could be her son's dad
Was just too sickening to comprehend
But boy did she miss a casual boyfriend
Little Jimmy sat staring in complete amazement
At the sea of Santas sprawled on the pavement

She returned to her car, got the engine started
But then the red sea of drunkenness parted
And there stood a dashing *'Santa Supreme'!*
With flowing white hair and eyes that did gleam
He walked towards her with a sober gait
His body carrying no extra weight

He was the buffest Santa she'd ever seen!
She hoped this encounter would not turn mean
As he looked her over, she started to blush
Like a schoolgirl with her first big crush
He apologised for his boorish brethren
And introduced himself by the name of Severen

Little Jimmy was equally enamoured
As Severen explained he does not get hammered
'Cause he's high on life and love for the Season
Bringing joy to the kids is his biggest reason
For joining this herd of misfit men
Maybe bring some stability to their pen

Lost in lust was Jimmy's mother
He certainly was not like any other
Santa. Even his clothing wasn't standard issue
She started to drool, he gave her a tissue
At this point she felt it only right
To offer him a ride, just to be polite

He accepted and hopped in the back seat
Smiling at Jimmy, who thought he was neat
She asked if he'd like to join them for dinner
Crossing her fingers she's on to a winner
He accepted again and said: "You're too kind"
But dinner wasn't what she had on her mind!

At the table he regaled them with stories
About the North Pole and all of its glories
Said he was a close friend of Santa, who's *real!*
And not just some fat guy who acts like a heel
Said he was privy to all of their wishes
As he cleared the table and washed the dishes

Jimmy's mother knew she had found 'Mr Right'
He told her 'twas fate that they met that night
They both put little Jimmy to bed
Severen gave him a wink, she kissed his forehead
Then she turned to Severen, acting all coy
He remarked, "Jimmy's a special little boy"

She smiled sweetly, growing weak at the knees
Thinking to herself, "Just take me *please!*"
He took her hand and she lead the way
To her bedroom where they could play
'What's in Santa Severen's sack?'
Once you go RED you never go back!

She removed his fitted suit of red leather
This could be her best Christmas *EVER!*
He whispered, "Your wishes are granted"
And with a thrust his festive seed he implanted
Now little Jimmy will have a father *and* brother!
And she'll forever be a Santa lover

Acknowledgements

* I'd like to thank the following people for their support with my efforts to complete this book:

June and Michael Llewellyn

Carole Tyrcha

Scott Kenemore [author]

Tim O'Donnell

Keenan Powell

* 'POET FOR SALE' - {pg. 11-13}, is available as a video performance free on YouTube:

https://youtu.be/xJzUvurDqIM

* Word art images by John Hain, free use via Pixabay.com:
pixabay.com/images/search/user:johnhain/

* I acknowledge that I procrastinated way too much on this collection.

Also by Claire Fluff Llewellyn

LOVE is a KILLER

An exploration into the dark depths of the fragile human heart, the twisted mind of love-crazed killers, and love-sick monsters!

Available on Amazon:

https://www.amazon.com/dp/1798690268

About the Author

Born June 1974 in Worcester, England, Claire Llewellyn first took an interest in poetry at an early age through primary school readings of Roald Dahl. She also developed a penchant for music, and the horror genre. Her schooling required her to write creatively in all formats and she soon acquired an affinity for it, constantly writing rhymes and short stories.

In her late teens, she pursued her musical interests and formed a band, 'Stir Crazy', performing classic rock covers and original material. She headed the band as lead vocalist and lyricist. When they disbanded, she bounced around musical groups and added the nickname "Fluff" as part of her persona in a new theatrical rock band venture that never came to fruition. However, it was her musical pursuits that lead her to move to Illinois in 2004.

As new opportunities arose, she became embroiled in a different kind of stage performance as an assistant to a Gothic illusionist. This adventure exposed her to the world of independent horror film making. She branched out into acting and ultimately formed her own small production company, 'Bloody Brit Productions', through which she directs her own screenplays.

This is her second publication of poetry, and quite different from the first which was horror themed. More collections are planned, especially in the horror realm. This departure from her usual genre, just felt right and is a nice variation, exposing her all around love for word play. Whilst fond of traditional rhyming verse, which she mostly ascribes to, maturity has afforded her the confidence to experiment a little. Poetry, and writing in general, has helped her through some tough times, allowing her to express difficult emotions, and even showcase that cheeky British humour.

www.ingramcontent.com/pod-product-compliance
Lightning Source LLC
Chambersburg PA
CBHW031258290426
44109CB00012B/643